a place called
Home

Dedication

Whole Home™ helps turn a house into a home. But for many women and children across Canada, a safe and comfortable home is only a dream. To help make their dream come true, we proudly dedicate *A Place Called Home* to these children and their families.

From the sale of every copy of this book, we put three dollars directly towards the provision of safe, temporary shelter for women and children in need.

To make this happen, Sears Whole Home™ has partnered with the YWCA of Canada. The YWCA works to meet the needs of women and their families in more than 200 communities coast to coast. Through its shelters across the country, the YWCA offers women and children in crisis a secure environment and helps them as they rebuild their lives.

For more information about the YWCA, its programs and its services, contact your local YWCA or reach the YWCA of Canada at (416) 962-8881 or www.ywcacanada.ca.

a place called Home

Lingo Media

Published for Sears Canada Inc. by:
Lingo Media
151 Bloor Street West
Suite 890
Toronto, ON
M5S 1S4

ISBN: 1-896391-63-X

Book concept and coordination team: Cheryl Grant, Sears Canada Inc.; Marilyn Toombs, Networks Studios; Susan Yates
Publisher: Susan Yates
Writer: Kathleen Crowley
Editor: Ilana Weitzman/Colborne Communications
Text and cover design: Dave Murphy/ArtPlus Limited
Page layout: Leanne O'Brien/ArtPlus Limited

Printed and bound in Canada

All the merchandise featured in *A Place Called Home*, except props and vintage items, is available from Sears Canada Inc.

Photography: Networks Studios

Contact:
Marilyn Toombs
15 Benton Road
Toronto, ON
M6W 3G2

Photography team: Mark Bradshaw, Michael Crichton, Shawn Harling, Shawn Hutchesen, Mehrab Moghadasia, Michael Nangroves, Mark Olsen, Agusto Rosales, Yoshi Wadano
Style director: Andrea McCrindle
Stylists: Louise Gregoire, Paula Taffa
Producer: Marianne Petroff

Whole Home stylists: Colleen Wittlin, Liz Bauer

Distributed by:
Sears Canada Inc.
222 Jarvis Street
Toronto, ON
M5B 2B8

TABLE OF CONTENTS

Come on in and Make Yourself at Home

Put up your feet and settle back with this fun, practical, richly illustrated book about how to make your home a beautiful place to live.

A Place Called Home delivers the best of today's concepts for home décor, with exciting ideas on how to express your own personal flair.

Creating a comfortable home isn't complicated or difficult. It's just a thoughtful blend of some of the basic principles discussed in this book: comfort, creativity, affordability, and quality. Whether you are trying to choose the perfect wall colour for a single room or furnish a home from top to bottom, these principles will help guide you towards choices that will transform any house into a place called home.

A Place Called Home was created by the fashion and design team of Sears Whole Home™. Whole Home™ is more than a brand of products. It is the philosophy of making a house into a home, affordably, through inspiring and coordinated décor.

It's a comfort to have a place to call home.

FACING PAGE *An easy chair, the warmth of sunlight, highly polished wood and an inviting bedroom all contribute towards home comfort.*

COMFORT

Comfort at home soothes the soul and pleases the body. When you decorate with comfort in mind, the choices you make reflect who you are.

Creating Comfort

Comfort should be the first and most important consideration for the place you call your own. After all, shouldn't it be a comfort to be home?

The starting point for creating comfort is the style, or type of décor, you choose. The easy-going style of "casual living," sometimes referred to as shabby chic or upscale country, is designed for maximum comfort. It's a simple and practical approach to home styling that's easy, relaxed and uncomplicated.

Casual living combines comfy furniture, subtle lighting, favourite colours and friendly textures. Geared toward comfort, it is a style that's designed to please, not to impress. The look and feel is loose, natural and pared down. Best of all, casual living doesn't have to be perfect. In fact, imperfection is part of its charm. Because it relaxes the rules, casual living is a flexible and forgiving way to decorate.

While traditional and contemporary styles create rooms that are elegant, graceful—and in the case of contemporary, spare—they often don't put comfort first. The traditional style tends to be formal, creating rooms that are meant more to be admired than lived-in. In contemporary designs, clean lines and stylized minimalism often take precedence over comfort.

Elements of both these styles can be mixed and matched with casual living. But when a room is designed for comfort, the kick-off-your-shoes and put-your-feet-up kind of feeling created by a casual living style can't be beat.

FACING PAGE *Casual living style is easy going. It combines comfy furnishings, good lighting and favourite colours to make the whole family feel right at home.*

Comfort with Casual Living Style

The signature of casual living is inviting furniture. Sofas are built to stretch out on. Chairs invite you to sink in and put your feet up. Generous ottomans do double duty as coffee tables and footstools. Hard angles are replaced by soft shapes and ample proportions: curved backs and arms, deep seats and plump cushions.

While there is nothing prim about a casual space, that doesn't mean you can't dress up the room for special occasions. In fact, the casual living style shifts easily from the informal to the elegant. Clutter can be conveniently stowed, lights dimmed, fresh flowers set out and candles lit. A casual room is a place where you can be equally comfortable curling up for an afternoon nap or welcoming friends for an evening celebration.

Casual living is a pared down and practical approach to styling. Stretch, curl, sprawl—feeling comfortable is your style.

THESE PAGES *A generous armchair and comfy throw create that put-up-your-feet feeling that defines comfort.*

Personal Comfort

Casual living is about creating comfortable, eclectic interiors that suit your own style.

The philosophy behind casual living is one of personal choice. The best casual spaces reveal the individuality and personality of their owners. Be guided by your own tastes and preferences, and surround yourself with what gives you comfort.

In casual living, you pull together the things you want, the way you want. Old and new, formal and informal, staid and off-the-wall all work together. A treasured quilt may be proudly placed on a table, or used as a window dressing. An informal dining set can sit comfortably in a sophisticated setting. And an old, well-loved chest can fit in just fine with more contemporary pieces.

It is the mix, not the match, that makes this style work.

FACING PAGE TOP *A charming new use for a favourite toy.*
BOTTOM *Design classics, like this vintage fan, are both functional and decorative.*
THIS PAGE TOP *Here's something to crow about: a weathered rooster sits happily by a well-loved country quilt.*
BOTTOM *If flowers aren't your style, a basket of fresh fruit is an edible alternative.*

7

Clutter-Control for Comfort

Casual living celebrates life-in-progress. A project underway on the dining room table, a book on the arm of a chair and a castle made of building blocks on the family room floor all speak of rooms that are happily lived-in.

Nevertheless, clutter has a way of taking over a space...a room...and even a home! Building clutter-control into your décor is essential. Baskets under tables, magazine racks, open shelving and closed cabinets are standard fixtures in casual living. They provide easy and accessible ways of keeping the things you want at hand—and neatly out of sight.

THESE PAGES *A stack of garage-sale suitcases makes for a quirky side table—and the perfect place to stash things away.*

A Comfortable Balance

A comfortable room is composed in a harmonious way. In the best rooms, no single piece overwhelms; instead, all the pieces work together. This harmony is achieved by balance and proportion.

The art of achieving balance begins with the consideration of space. In smaller rooms, less is more: aim for a sense of spaciousness instead of tightly packing the room with big furniture. In big rooms, big pieces generate excitement—think baby grand piano!—but larger rooms also need the balance of intimacy for comfort.

Scale also plays a role in harmonious design. Furniture that's too big or too small for the size of the room, or in relation to the other pieces, will make a room uncomfortable. So too will an arrangement that's off-kilter. Simple fixes can help re-balance a room. A piece considerably larger than the other furnishings will look better simply by placing a proportionately sized plant next to it. Similarly, a small piece that looks lost and out of place can be comfortably balanced by grouping it with other "like" pieces.

In combination with space and scale, the shape and features of a room—its windows, doorways and wall spaces—also help to dictate a balanced arrangement of furnishings. A circle of armchairs or two love seats facing one another will look better and feel more comfortable in a small room than a three-seater couch that's been squeezed in. Remember that the rooms are yours: focus on making them comfortable for you.

FACING PAGE *A symmetrical design brings peace and a sense of space to a small living room.*

Lighting for Comfort

When it comes to the details of a room, lighting is fundamental. Good lighting adds depth, warmth, tone and texture. A comfortably lit room has a variety of types and sources of light, including natural light, task lighting and indirect light.

Natural light enhances the appearance of a room and adds to its energy and warmth. It can be celebrated with stained glass and uncovered windows. For best effect, however, even natural light should be controlled. Sheer drapes soften, shutters and louvres add drama, and blinds and draperies can screen light entirely.

The time of day and the season affect the quantity and quality of natural light in a room. Morning light may be welcome, but the hard sun of late afternoon can feel hot and draining. Window direction or shade from a large tree can also make a big difference. So, too, will the season. The light streaming through a large south-facing window will be very different in July than in January.

Natural light in a room should always be supplemented by artificial light. A well-lit work surface, a bright bathroom mirror and a proper reading lamp are not just niceties— they are necessities. Good task lighting lets you pursue life's activities with ease and comfort.

Indirect lighting from floor, table, pendant and chandelier lights can enhance the style, shape and mood of a room. Well-placed lights—and well-chosen bulbs—can help diminish faults, highlight features and change atmosphere.

FACING PAGE *Good lighting can make a room. Use a variety of light sources to create impact and to best suit the task at hand.*

Natural Light

Sunlight creates wonderfully comfortable places in a home. A bright kitchen boosts energy at the start of the day. A sunny, warm nook is perfect for indulging in afternoon naps. And a dusky place provides space for quiet contemplation.

Window coverings are like a dimmer switch for natural light—for maximum wattage, use them sparingly or use light-weight sheers. To turn down the glare, use fabric, wooden shutters or blinds.

AT RIGHT *Natural light is warm and inviting. Every room should make the most of available natural light.*

Task Lighting

Whether you are reading a book, chopping vegetables or applying make-up, good lighting is essential. Decisions about task lighting will always be driven by practicality, but there is room for good looks as well.

Directional pot lights, track lights, pendant lights, clamp lights and lamps with moveable arms are all options for task lighting.

The aim of task lighting is to create sufficient, focused light without shadow. For a kitchen work surface, a desk, a stairwell or a reading area, light should fall in front of—not directly in—the eyes. In the bathroom, where there is a need for shadow-free light, illumination should come from beside—not above—the eyes. Lights beside the mirror accomplish this.

Different types of light bulbs can create varying qualities of light. Halogen lamps give off a clear, white light that is most like daylight. Regular incandescent bulbs cast yellow light. Fluorescent bulbs give off a bluish light.

Comfortable task lighting lets you accomplish the job at hand safely and easily.

FACING PAGE *Task lighting is focussed lighting. It is essential to have adequate task lighting in the working rooms of the house: the kitchen and bathroom. Good task lighting makes the difference between a comfy armchair and a comfy armchair where you can settle down for a good read.*

Indirect Lighting

 Indirect lighting is like mood music. It lets you set the tone of the moment: a soft glow for intimate dining, a play of light and shadow for dramatic effects, mellow candlelight for relaxation and bright light as an antidote to the darkness of winter.

Different directions and intensities of light can soften the edges in a room. Light can also lend definition and accentuate proportion. The variety and combination of lighting options helps create the effect you want, whether it be uplights for drama and emphasis, pooled light to cast a glow or wall washers for soft background.

Achieving your desired effect with a lighting scheme comes about through experimentation. It doesn't have to be complicated. A dimmer switch, for instance, is a simple way to alter mood and create comfort.

THESE PAGES *Indirect light is softer than task lighting. It can be dramatic—as these grouped candles illustrate—or diffused, as in the light of a chandelier with individual lamp shades.*

Colour for Comfort

Colour has an enormous impact on the way we feel. It's what makes the first impression in any room. Colour pulls us in and makes us want to stay.

The science of colour studies the effects of colour on mood and atmosphere. For example, colours in the red-to-yellow spectrum make us feel comfortable and secure. Known as the sun colours, they give a room a welcoming glow and we associate them with pleasure.

By contrast, the so-called water colours of the blue-green spectrum are known to produce feelings of renewal and calm.

You can create comfort not only through your choice of colour, but also through the way you use it. Monochromatic schemes use just one colour, in various tones and intensities. A monochromatic scheme that uses calm colours, such as off-whites or greens, will create a sense of soothing comfort. The gentle variations in shade and tone produce an overall feeling of serenity.

Ultimately, in the relaxed style of casual living, choosing a comfortable colour comes down to you. We all have our own colour associations. Some colours just feel right to us. So choose colours to which you're naturally drawn and strike out on your own, even if it means an unconventional colour choice.

FACING PAGE *The bright colours in this jug of flowers add vibrancy to the room. Colour is a highly personal choice that works best when it just feels right.*

Colour
It Warm

Deep rich red, earthy terra cotta, buttery yellow—these are the full and mellow colours of the warm palette that draw us into a room. They can create a cozy, intimate feeling or stimulate the senses. Warm colours evoke the warmth and energy of the sun.

These joyful colours are particularly well suited to the kitchen and dining room. A soft yellow gives off a warm glow, even on a cloudy day. A dramatic red flatters skin tones and creates a sense of intimacy. It stimulates conversation. Terra cotta anchors a room with a solid, comforting feeling.

Warm colours envelop a space and create wraparound comfort.

THESE PAGES *Red tones used in a dining room will be warm and inviting, and stimulate the appetite!*

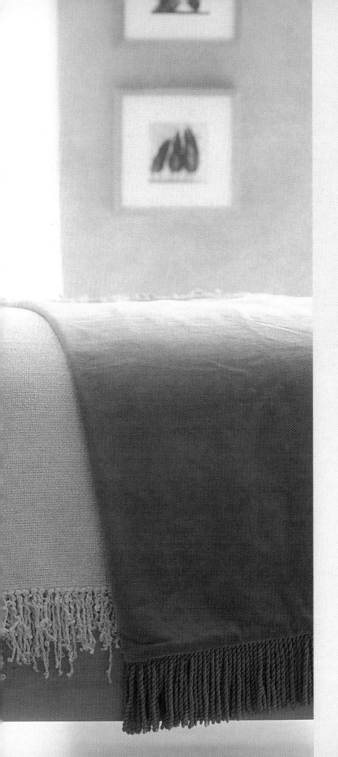

Colour It Calm

For many, a monochromatic room in calming colours is the perfect respite from the stressful world outside. The use of one basic colour creates a backdrop for a room free of distractions. Subtle variations in shade and texture add interest and dimension. The overall effect stills the senses and clears the mind.

The calming effect of monochromatic schemes makes them ideally suited to bedrooms and living rooms. Creamy whites, mochas and vanillas have a muted and luminous quality. The colours of the cool palette—watery shades of lilac, pale blues and greens—act like a refreshing tonic.

A monochromatic scheme, painted in a calming colour, is a simple way to create a tranquil refuge in your home.

AT LEFT *Blonde woods and natural materials are at home in a calming colour scheme.*

Colour
It Mine

How do you begin to pick colour for your home?

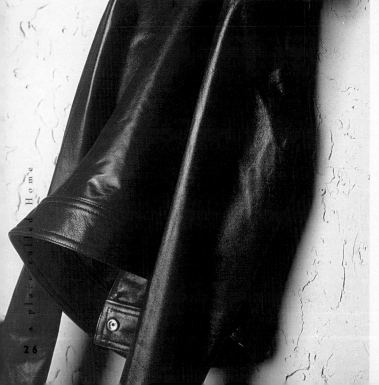

A good place to start is with colours that you like. Take a second look at the pages in decorating magazines that catch your eye. Do those pages have a certain fundamental colour in common? Likewise, think about your wardrobe or your garden. Is there a repeated colour? Gauge your response to colour. Is there a colour that makes you happy? Answers to these questions will help you pick colours that you feel naturally comfortable with.

a place called Home

More and more, colours like purple, hot pink, lime green and denim blue are crossing over from the closet to the couch, becoming statements in home fashion. But colour choice goes beyond trends. For a colour to be an enduring part of your home, it should make you feel at home, reflecting you and your tastes.

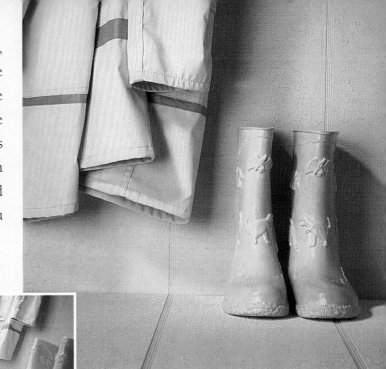

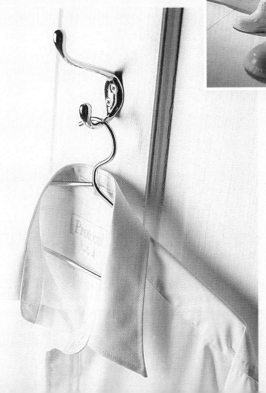

We all have colours that please us. Take inspiration where you find it and go with your favourites.

THESE PAGES

*If you're having trouble choosing a colour
for your home, look to your wardrobe.
Chances are if you love to wear a colour,
you will probably love to live with it.*

Comfortable Favourites

Collecting was once reserved for objects of substance: art works, stamps or rare coins. Now, collecting has become a more down-to-earth business that happily includes everything from teddy bears to teapots.

Collectors or not, we all have at least a few favourite things. Whether it is a porch rocker from grandma's house, an old teddy that shared childhood secrets, a collection of family photos or trinkets from an exotic trip, these treasures say something about who we are. It's a comfort to have them around us.

Comfort comes from the familiar, from things that don't change, from things we can depend on. Children are enormously comforted by well-loved, old blankets. Grown-ups, too, find comfort in favourite and familiar things. These mementos have the ability to transport us to another time and place. A favourite old quilt, for example, wraps up memories that go far beyond its constituent pieces of cloth and stuffing.

Collections personalize and humanize our rooms and keep them from being too stiff. Each treasured object contains a story—a bit of history or a reflection of a hobby or interest—that reveals something of the collector.

We derive comfort from being surrounded by things that give us pleasure. Including them in our homes gives us a sense of ourselves and a sense of continuity.

FACING PAGE *Personal treasures that reveal something of you transform a house into a home.*

How Comfort Feels

Texture gives sensation to a room. It is the feeling underfoot, the touch of fabrics, the look of smooth or rough surfaces. By going beyond the sense of sight, texture allows for a deeper connection with our living space.

From a scratchy sisal carpet on the floor to the nap of velvet on a favourite chair, texture can be used throughout a room to add depth and life. Texture can be rough or smooth, warm or cool, soft or hard. Think of texture as you choose your materials. Finding contrasts in texture is essential to add real dimension to a room.

Texture can also be used to create a specific mood in a room. There are textures that are decidedly feminine, such as lace, and those that are tailored to the masculine, like rough leather. Texture can make a bedroom romantic with delicate organza and lacy fabrics, a den masculine with hard woods and crafted leather or a kitchen cozy with pine wainscotting and floors.

While texture caters to the sense of touch, it also adds comfort by connecting us to a room on a number of levels. Texture gives quality to colour and light. It creates depth in pattern and dimension in colour. The texture of a waffle weave, for example, brings plain beige to life. A smooth silk drape ripples with light and shadow. Variations in texture keep a monochromatic colour scheme from being lifeless by giving it dimension.

Texture is an important element in creating comfort. Its sensuality brings rooms to life.

FACING PAGE *Texture adds definition to a room.*
Combining a variety of textures adds interest and invites touch.

Comfort Fabrics

The texture of cloth can add another layer of comfort to a room. Soft, thick knits and nubbly weaves are warm and welcoming. Smooth, cool-to-the-touch materials like cotton or satin have a soothing, contemplative effect. A quilted cushion gives you hands-on pleasure. Cozy fabrics like chenille are synonymous with comfort.

Think, too, about how fabric can alter the tone of a room. A touch of lace can balance the functional nature of the bathroom or soften the rigid lines of an imposing sideboard. Sheer curtains on a window can transform the landscape beyond.

THESE PAGES *From the charms of a textured cotton coverlet to the comfort of a fuzzy angora throw, texture enriches just about any fabric.*

Finishes
for Comfort

Floors and walls are the "bones" of a home and define the size, shape and even purpose of rooms. But they are also surfaces to play with, and can add visual and textural interest to a space.

Finishes soften or harden a room. Imperfect finishes add character, lending a room an old and well-loved look. In contrast, the lack of detail in "perfect" finishes gives a room a more clean, contemporary feel.

Aged wood floorboards, with all their bumps, grooves and blemishes, are probably the ultimate in imperfect finishes. With so much history underfoot, rooms with old floorboards give us a comforting sense of continuity and endurance.

A deep, plush carpet—one of the perfect finishes—can also add much to a room by softening hard edges and muffling sound. Sisal and seagrass are natural finishes that lie somewhere between the two.

Marble, ceramic tile and glossy walls harden the look. A roughly plastered wall—evocative of the Mediterranean—and smooth, matte walls soften a room.

Finishes are one of the building blocks of comfort.

THESE PAGES

FACING PAGE TOP *A sisal mat is a natural finish that can add warmth to a room.* **BOTTOM** *Glazed walls are an imperfect finish that is forgiving.* **THIS PAGE TOP** *A fresco on a roughly finished wall adds character to a room.* **BOTTOM** *Natural finishes, like this mat and stone floor, add visual and textural interest to the space.*

a place called Home

Forgive and Forget

Living is comfortable when the maintenance is easy. Opt for forgiving materials and finishes that look good as they age.

Pine is more tolerant of dust, dents and fingerprints than high-gloss wood. Wood is more forgiving than glass. Looped carpeting, like berber, and natural rugs, such as sisal, are highly wearable and easy to maintain. Oriental and patterned carpets can hide a multitude of sins. In general, wood floors with area rugs are easier to maintain than wall-to-wall carpeting. On walls, satin finish paints withstand more wiping than flat.

When you're designing for comfort, factor appearance and practicality into the equation.

THESE PAGES *Easy-to-care for walls, floors and furniture are low maintenance and easy to live with.*

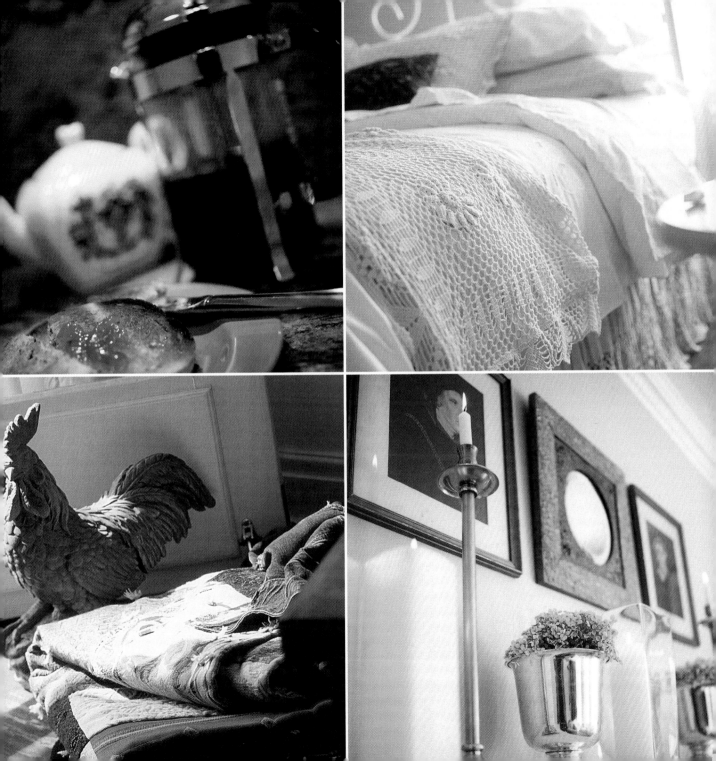

CREATIVITY

Great ideas aren't reserved for style gurus. From magazines to books to the homes of friends and family, we're surrounded by sources of inspiration. All you need to do is make them your own.

◆

Creativity Basics

We tend to think of creativity as being something natural— you either have it or you don't. But being creative doesn't  mean being an original or being the first to try something. It does mean being able to recognize a good idea when you see it and, then, to modify it and adapt it in your own way.

Clever decorating ideas can come from many different places. To get your creativity flowing, visit showrooms, follow trends in decorating magazines and seek out designer showcases. Get a feel for what professionals are doing and what fabrics, materials and finishes are available.

Begin with floors, walls and windows. With creative treatment, they can be elevated from background to statement. Try floor coverings and finishes that are forgiving, while highly individual. Cover walls with more than just a coat of paint—hang an old quilt or antique map for interest and impact. Adorn your windows with coverings that have the power to play with the sun and create illusions.

Keep on the lookout for inspiration for your home and explore as many creative ideas as you can.

FACING PAGE *The best design ideas are often the result of unusual combinations of everyday things, such as this tea towel that doubles as a window covering.*

Creativity
Beneath
Your Feet

Creative floor coverings and finishes can be used to give a room a new look, add interest, direct traffic flow, make a statement and define space.

Area rugs are wonderfully adaptable and useful. In a big room, a rug can define space, creating a room within a room. Rugs can also give better proportion to a room—for instance, by squaring up a narrow space. Small area rugs can accentuate a focal point such as a fireplace.

Painting wood or linoleum floors can produce amazing effects. A checkerboard pattern painted in black and white, or dark green and white, can formalize a hallway or dining room. A border stencilled directly onto the floor effectively directs traffic. When used in a child's bedroom, the floor treatment can keep pace with the growing child. Teddy bears make way for a face-off circle!

THESE PAGES *It's a jungle in here! The floor, walls and even shutters get creative treatment in this child's room.*

Off the Wall

Think of a wall as a blank canvas. Since walls are one of the easiest surfaces to change, they're the perfect place to be creative—without much risk. Offer up a daily menu of food and inspiration on a blackboard wall in your kitchen or bathroom.

Hang a tapestry in your living room. Liven up a kitchen backsplash with a few hand-painted tiles. Glue large old murals, newspapers or maps onto the walls of a home study or library to lend a scholarly and thoughtful air.

You can use paints, faux finishes, paper, wood, tile or fabric to create the effects you want. Apply them on their own or in combination to add drama, make a theme come alive or enhance the mood of a room.

It's even an option to leave your walls blank! As a backdrop, unadorned walls can showcase your best prints, paintings and collections. Instead of a special paint finish, try a bulletin-board scrapbook to liven up your surroundings.

THESE PAGES *Walls offer lots of creative possibilities. Paint can be applied over almost any surface, such as (this page, bottom) wood panelling and (facing page) brick.*

Creative
Windows

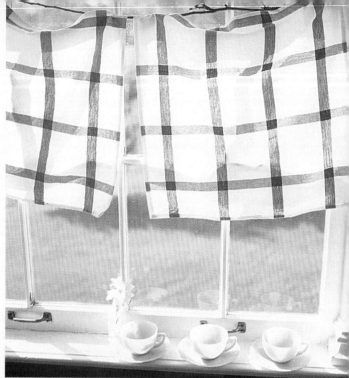

Our eyes are naturally drawn to windows. Windows are not only an important source of light, but also link the interior with the world outside. So don't just cover them up—windows are a great spot for creative treatments and individual expression.

The challenge for window treatments is to maximize natural light while maintaining privacy. Café curtains—also called half curtains—cover the bottom half of the window while allowing light to stream in from above. Blinds that can be raised or lowered are also a good solution.

Window treatments can diminish or augment the proportions of a window. Mounting a curtain track above a window, for instance, will make it appear taller.

The creativity of a window covering may be in the detail—an interesting rod, finial or tieback. You can also experiment with trim. Buttons, fringes and contrasting borders each add an unexpected element to ordinary curtains.

Or try the unconventional. A room screen is both an unusual and an effective way to create privacy; a sunny window can become a greenhouse with glass shelves and pots of herbs or flowers.

THESE PAGES

Windows are a great spot for creative treatment. Try a simple window screen made of tea towels, jars of flowers on a windowsill, a touch of lace or frames of pressed leaves.

Creativity in Focus

Every major room needs a focal point—the place to which our eyes are naturally drawn. Focal points provide visual satisfaction. They define furniture arrangement and determine traffic flow. Best of all, a focal point anchors an entire room.

While some of us may have an ornate mantel or stained glass window, a focal point doesn't always naturally occur in a room. That's when it's up to you to create one.

A piece of furniture with great presence or novelty can serve as a focal point. So, too, can showcased art, such as a dramatic painting or sizable sculpture. A grand mirror propped against a wall or a stunning floral arrangement is also effective.

Even natural focal points need creative emphasis to draw attention to their role in the room. A fireplace needs a mantel display. A dramatic view requires lots of exterior lights at night to maintain the effect.

Group your furniture away from the focal point so as not to obstruct it from view. Likewise, to emphasize architectural elements such as French doors, keep them in a clear line of vision. Window coverings and furniture arrangements must work together to draw the eye to such features as a stunning window.

It's important to keep balance in play and not have more than one focal point in a room. Otherwise the room will have an unsettled feel while the eye searches for a place to rest.

FACING PAGE *A Japanese-influenced arrangement provides focus in a contemporary room.*

Creativity with Colour

Choosing colours from all the shades, tones, combinations and variations available can be daunting. A basic understanding of colour theory is the surest springboard to good creative combinations.

The colour wheel forms the basis of colour theory. It is anchored by the three primary colours—red, yellow and blue. Primary colours are pure colours, meaning they cannot be created through any combination of other colours. All of the other colours are made through combinations of the primary colours—orange from red and yellow, green from blue and yellow, and so on.

Colours are roughly grouped into harmonious, complementary and toning colours. Harmonious colours are the progressive shades between primary colours such as orange, which falls between red and yellow. Complementary colours are opposite each other on the wheel. They combine with dramatic effect—poppy red with turquoise, for instance, or orange with deep blue. Toning colours are the variations of shades within one colour group. When used together, toning colours create a calming, monochromatic effect.

White and black are achromatic colours. In combination with other colours, white lightens and softens. Black darkens, defines and adds detail. Achromatic colours work in harmonious, complementary and toning combinations. The diluted tones between black and white—bone, beige and gray—combine well as harmonious colours and are equally effective in monochromatic schemes.

Colour is somewhat relative. The way we see a colour is affected by surrounding colours, texture and light. For example, yellow placed next to white appears to blend into the white, diluting the colour. The same yellow pops out brightly in company with black.

Colours look different in natural light, at different times of day and under different light conditions. That's why it's important to experiment with the placement of a colour and observe it at different times of day before you commit to a choice.

Within the colour spectrum, warm colours like reds, oranges, yellows and dark browns enclose a space. Cool colours that reflect light—such as pale greens, blues and lilacs—tend to recede in a room and create a feeling of spaciousness.

A grasp of the basics of colour sets the scene for their creative use. Colour is tremendously versatile. It can be used in harmonious, complementary or toning variations to define a space, to form a subtle background, to accent a room or to create the illusion of more space or less.

The colours that will work best in your home are those that come from your preferred palette. If you don't have defined tastes already, make a point of noticing how different colours affect you. What sensation do colours evoke for you? Are you naturally drawn to specific colours? What kind of effect would you like to create?

AT RIGHT *For a decorator look, consider how all the elements that go into a room can be used to contribute colour.*

Colour Magic

Colour creates illusion. It can open a space up or pull it in and make it appear smaller.

Light colours create the impression of light, airy space. Used on the walls, ceiling and floor, the room will seem larger because there are no clear lines of definition. Light colours are a good choice for basements, which are generally cursed with little natural light and low ceilings. They're also a good way to create a feeling of spaciousness in small powder rooms and entranceways.

When you want to make a room more intimate, warm colours like reds and yellows will make it appear smaller. A darker paint on the ceiling will make it appear lower.

Continuity with Colour

Colour forges links both within rooms and throughout the home. Finding colours that harmonize creates continuity in home décor.

If your colour scheme is seemingly at odds, you can pull it together by establishing a thread of colour that runs throughout the room or house. Colour can also be used to accent the relationship between rooms: a doorway in a complementary colour can frame a colourful vista beyond.

Colour links need not be reserved for walls. Accessories, such as a throw rug in a doorway or a picture in a hallway, can foreshadow colours to come. Big pillar candles or a grouping of tapers can create a colour link that's easy to try and change at whim.

A coordinated colour scheme can be very useful at pulling together dissimilar furnishings. Because the eye is drawn to the colours instead of the shapes or form of the furniture, even mismatched pieces seem to fit together.

THESE PAGES *Colours that harmonize will create continuity between rooms.*

Accent with Colour

There's nothing like a splash of colour to punctuate a room, be it vibrant cushions on a plain sofa or a contrasting trim around a window. Creative accent colour injects life and personality into a room.

Accents work not only for this jolt of liveliness, but also to enhance and balance other colours or features in a room. If you've chosen a complementary colour scheme, for example, you won't want to use the colours in equal measures or they will compete. In a sunflower yellow room, accent touches of aubergine—in lampshades, cushions and table accessories—complement without competing.

Accent colours in area rugs, cushions and artwork enliven neutral furniture and unify a room. They can also add interest and enhance a colour scheme. In a light room, dark wooden accents—such as shutters, artifacts and chair frames—contrast the airy quality of the space, preventing the room from feeling too cold in winter.

THESE PAGES *Use lively colour accents to inject life and personality against natural wood tones.*

Décor @ Work

Home décor is partly about adapting to changes in lifestyle. When a home office is needed or a new hobby takes over, single-purpose rooms can be easily converted to dual-use space.

For rooms that serve as both office and living space, the challenge is to be able to shift easily from the efficient and functional to the intimate and relaxing. You should be able to work in privacy, but also be able to close the door on work at day's end. Flexibility and organization are two key ways to create a successful office in the home.

A good starting point is furniture. Furnishings in a home office have to work extra hard—they must add to the look of the room and camouflage work-in-progress when needed. A handsome armoire, for instance, can disguise a workstation while housing all the necessary equipment: computer, fax and filing system.

A room screen creates privacy during working hours and blocks work from view after hours. Computer carts and filing cabinets on wheels are versatile solutions that allow work to be wheeled out of sight.

Chic accessories can be at home both at work and at play. An attractive clock, a water jug and glasses on a tray, flowers and containers with lids easily cross over from work space to living space. Ingenious accessories can also do double duty to transform a space, such as a bulletin board that can be turned over to reveal an attractive print.

FACING PAGE *Lunch break! Smart chairs around a modern table are comfortable for both working and casual dining. The armoire hides the computer to make the dining room dual purpose.*

a place called Home

Creating Space

Furniture and space pose one of those chicken-and-egg questions: furniture defines space, but space dictates furniture. Which comes first?

Space is, ultimately, the dictating force. The trick is to find furniture to accommodate the space you have.

Start by thinking about how the room will be used and organize around the practical first, making full use of horizontal and vertical space. For example, a "loft" bunk with a desk below makes a small bedroom bigger. Tall shelving units make use of space up to the ceiling. Layered furniture, like hassocks under a table or nesting tables, gives you extra furnishings when needed without cramping day-to-day style.

In a large, open space such as a loft, begin by carving out spaces within the room. Use big pieces to divide a room for multiple uses. Room screens can be used to create separate spaces that will make a big space more intimate.

AT RIGHT *Fabric panels, drapes or this bright sari are ways to enclose a space that can easily be drawn back to open the room up when needed.*

a place called Home

Show Off!

Collections and personal treasures put an imprint on a home. Whether your tastes run to figurines or botanical prints, displaying them creatively will really show them off.

Coffee tables, mantels, windowsills, shelves and walls can all be used for creative displays. On surfaces, group similar objects together with attention to contrasts in colour, size and texture. Break up large collections and play with combinations for impact. You might, for example, alternate books and pottery on a shelving unit. Give pride of place to one special item, either through lighting or by making it the focal point of an arrangement. Arrange smaller items so that they are grouped together, perhaps on a tray or in a special display unit.

Walls in every part of the house can be part of your personal gallery. A bathroom, hallway or a narrow wall between windows might be perfect for a collection of pictures, prints or personal treasures. Aligning a collection of same-size pictures—such as botanicals or black-and-white photos—heightens the overall effect. With hangings of varying size, group collections fairly close together. Individual pieces in a grouping should have some affinity for one another, so consider the balance and content of the group before hammering in the first nail.

Straw hats in a hallway, fishing tackle in a family room, and menus, postcards, old calendars and children's masterpieces all add new dimension to otherwise empty spaces.

FACING PAGE *When you're charmed by the face of an old clock or the patina on a trophy, chances are visitors will be too.*

Creativity with the Seasons

Keeping your décor in step with the seasons gives your home a chance to create itself anew.

Small adjustments revitalize a space without much fuss. In hallways, family rooms and living rooms, seasonal flowers and displays freshen the look. Changing the weight and colour of throws, decorative cushions and area rugs is an easy way to match the season. In the summer, pack away accessories to give rooms a fresh, clean, uncluttered look. Lighten up bedrooms in hot weather by packing away wooly blankets and duvets in favour of cool coverlets, and change towels in the bath to white or cool blue.

Give special consideration to your focal point. If it's the fireplace, a large, lacy fern keeps the otherwise "dead" firebox attractive, even when the season doesn't call for a twinkling fire.

Consider, too, the seasonal quality of lighting. Hot weather calls for minimal lighting. But when chill winds blow, it's time to bring on all the warm lighting effects you can muster.

THESE PAGES *The same dishes are easily adapted to each season by clever accessorizing.*

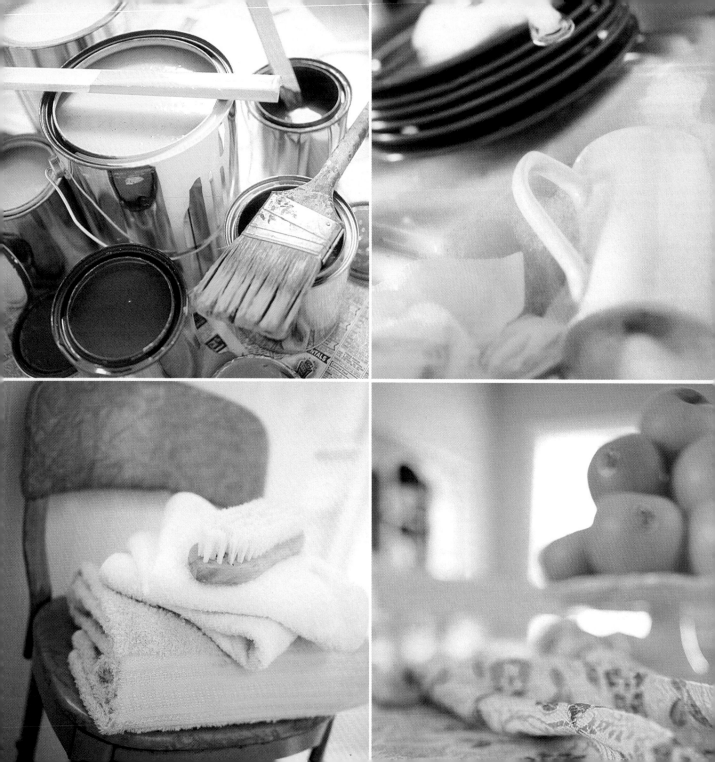

AFFORDABILITY

A comfortable home evolves over time. Rather than following trends, the most enduring homes are aligned with the needs, personal tastes and budget of the owners.

Planning

A home is a work-in-progress. Even if there are no budget restrictions when it comes to furnishing and decorating, it's a good idea to live in a home for a while before making changes. You'll be able to get a feel for the place and allow your dream plan to evolve over time.

As a starting point, keep a home journal where you can draw your rooms to scale. Evaluate each room's features. Then, begin to imagine what décor, colours, textures and lighting you want. Save pictures from catalogues and magazines, and add in colour chips and fabric swatches that appeal to you.

Then comes the time of reckoning, when you have to balance dreams with dollars.

Begin by dividing your wish list into three categories: essential, preferred and deluxe. The bare essentials for any home are good beds, comfortable seating, task lighting, and tables and chairs for dining. Put your money into these important pieces, then accessorize around them. Don't spend a lot of money on accent pieces. Always opt for quality over quantity.

First purchases can be earmarked for other uses down the road. You can start with a pine table in the dining room and eventually move it into the kitchen. Likewise, starter living room purchases can someday be retired to the family room. Choosing initial purchases in neutral colours will give you more options later on.

FACING PAGE *A scrapbook of home décor ideas, including paint chips, magazine clippings and other samples, can be a continuing source of inspiration.*

what about leather?

Consider:

• Leather is not only soft and sensuous, it is
  practical and durable, practically impossible to
  wear out.

• ... her repels liquids and stains, requiring little
  ... beyond a damp cloth.

• ... stays pliable for years, resisting ...

• ... actually getting softer and more ...
  with age as the oils from your skin ...
  ... character and patina. ...

• ... her" and adjusts to body ...
  ... both in

• Who will be using ...

• How long do you expect the sofa to last?

• Are you replacing only the sofa? (A new sofa can
  make everything else in the room look a bit faded
  and worn.)

• Look for a sofa that addresses all the considerations
  listed above.

• Make sure the spring construction provides adequa...
  supp...

• For firm..., look for a kiln-dried hardwood frame ...
  ... rewed reinforcement blocks.

• ... on fir... sofa. Get comfortable on it ...
  ... padding on the arm of the sofa, the bette...

• ... ake home samples of upholstery and look at the
  colours under different lighting conditions.

Versatile Décor

Looking at how your family really moves through your home can inspire new uses for rooms. Lots of functional, versatile and affordable furnishings are available to help you get the most mileage from your space.

The way to get maximum use out of a room is to analyze your family's true needs. List all the things you might do in a given space. Then, as you plan, incorporate solutions that allow the room to shift easily from one use to another.

When space is at a premium, many rooms have dual functions. A guest bedroom will serve as a den, a kitchen as a study hall and a dining room as a home office. Today's homes maximize furnishings through multi-functional pieces while minimizing clutter.

Multi-functional furniture adds style and flexibility to a room. This includes furniture designed for multiple uses, furniture that moves from room to room and furniture that keeps work or televisions out of sight when need be.

Storage becomes more important in dual-purpose rooms. Creative shelving can serve as both a décor feature and a practical means of organizing clutter. Containers are an indispensable way to keep necessities on hand but hidden away. Storage works best when it is decorative as well as useful.

FACING PAGE TOP *A long sofa table does double duty for buffet dining.*
BOTTOM *A sofa bed easily transforms a family room to an extra bedroom.*

Clever
Disguises

All is not necessarily what it seems in the world of furniture. Many pieces cleverly hide multiple personalities. The sofa bed is a classic example. More surprising conversions include elegant hall chests that fold into single beds, shelving units that hinge down to become tables, and tables and ottomans that open into chests.

Such convertible pieces allow you to maximize the use of your space. So does furniture that provides for multiple activities. An armoire that conceals a television, stereo or workstation can allow the room to be used for another purpose. In the bedroom, small chests of drawers are a smart alternative to bedside tables.

Double-duty furniture gives you two pieces of furniture for the price of one. Now that's affordable.

THESE PAGES *Hide-and-seek? No one would ever guess that this elegant cabinet shown in the small photos at right hides a bed inside.*

Storage Solutions

When you add attractive storage to your décor, you achieve two ends: organization and decoration.

Free-standing shelf-racks and pot hangers in the kitchen can take the place of expensive cabinetry. Shelves filled with rolled towels in the bathroom are a pretty and practical feature.

Wall-to-wall bookcases create space for books, games, crafts and treasures.

Baskets and plastic containers are affordable, good-looking receptacles for just about anything. The only caveat: open-topped containers must be large enough to hide their contents from view.

When you look for storage options, don't overlook any surface. A plate rail in a child's room is the perfect place to show off stuffed animals. A shelf supported by beautiful brackets positioned about a foot below the ceiling can become a wonderful place to display treasured objects.

Tidying up clutter with storage solutions is one of the easiest ways to bring a sense of peace and calm to a room.

FACING PAGE *Don't overlook the unusual when looking for storage.*
Fruit crates and baskets make excellent containers.

Quick Fixes

A little ingenuity can create some of the most
cheerful—and cheap—decorating solutions.
A personal touch, a coat of paint or a well-
placed plant can renew the look of a room.

Accessories make a house instantly feel like a home. Pictures and collections that reveal your personality give a room a comfortable feel. And the accessories themselves can be inexpensive—a collection of rocks, a bouquet of daisies, jars of preserves. Scented candles create instant atmosphere.

A fresh coat of paint is one of the most economical ways to make over a room. A change in background colour, a special effect or a lick of paint on an old piece of wooden furniture can do wonders for a room.

The addition of plants is another affordable way to breathe life into a room. Greenery adds warmth, texture, shape and drama. Plants can buffer sound, direct traffic, balance empty spaces and replace drapery as an inexpensive privacy screen. A single bloom will punctuate a space with colour.

The very best rooms are often the result of thoughtful touches—not big budgets.

FACING PAGE TOP LEFT *A teacup collection is lovingly displayed on a windowsill.*
TOP RIGHT *A painted shelf is far more interesting by the addition of colour.*
BOTTOM RIGHT *A tea towel is a charming choice for a kitchen table runner.*
BOTTOM LEFT *Collectable dishes put to new uses make instant organizers.*

Accessories on a Shoestring

Natural objects make interesting and affordable accessories, and are right at home in casual living décor. Rock collections, curlicue branches and dried flowers can be shown off on windowsills, coffee tables and sideboards.

Use what naturally belongs in a room to dress it up. Interesting spice containers, jars of preserves, bottles of oils and vinegars and pretty platters of fruit add charm and flair to a kitchen. Crisp tea towels make inexpensive napkins for a casual get-together. Colourful soaps, shells and rolled towels add personality in the bathroom.

a place called Home

Found objects have décor impact and the warm memories that come from finding them. Smooth river stones can be piled into a rough hewn bowl. Flowers, such as hydrangea, can be dried for a magnificent floral arrangement, while others, such as roadside daisies or black-eyed Susan make lovely framed specimens when they have been pressed.

FACING PAGE **TOP** *Beautiful jars of jams and preserves create an eye-catching display.* **BOTTOM** *Yesterday's suitcases make a great side table, inside or out.* **THIS PAGE** **TOP** *Be versatile when you look for creative solutions. Old tin cans can be pressed into service as vases.* **BOTTOM** *Clothespins tacked into the wall are excellent to use for your own personal photo gallery.*

The Glory
of Paint

Paint is a wonderful decorating tool. It's relatively inexpensive, easy to apply, easy to change and comes in colours to suit any and every taste.

Paint a wall, a door, an old table or a chair and you have transformed the room. A flea market find becomes a treasure with a coat of paint. A dull room can be made lively with a fresh new colour. For impact, paint a ceiling sunshine yellow or lighten dark kitchen cabinets with a coat of soft, sage green.

Not only colour, but different paint techniques create special moods in a room. Stencils range from country floral to formal. Rough finishes give a room an old-world feel.

Paint is the great transformer. It's the fastest and cheapest way to change the personality of a room.

FACING PAGE Rejuvenating spa or elegant powder room? What a difference a coat of paint makes changing this room! *THIS PAGE* Instant makeover: new fabric and paint transforms this tag sale chair from country charmer to elegant diner.

QUALITY

There is sheer delight in having fine things. When you buy well,
you are choosing quality that will last.

◆

Quality Underfoot

When you lay the groundwork for quality in your home, start with the carpet, wood or tiles underfoot. Top-quality choices in flooring will deliver good looks that last.

There are two types of wooden flooring for home use: solid wood and laminated wood. Solid wood is the usual choice for living rooms, dining rooms, family rooms and bedrooms. Laminated wood floors are more forgiving of moisture and temperature variations, making them a better choice for kitchens, bathrooms and basements. The most common woods used for flooring are oak, maple and pine. Each offers a distinctive colour, grain and lustre.

Wool sets the standard in carpeting. It is highly durable, stain and soil resistant, and very resilient. The number of tufts per square inch and the height of the pile indicate quality. A wool and nylon blend combines looks with durability. With blends, less than 20 percent in content of any one fibre has no effect on overall carpet quality.

The best area rugs are hand-woven wool carpets such as Oriental rugs and kilims. Quality is designated by knots per square inch with hand-knotted rugs. Such rugs are investments that can be moved from home to home, and passed from generation to generation.

The quality of soft-tile flooring such as cork, vinyl and rubber is gauged by its thickness, resiliency and underlay. Hard-tile flooring such as marble, ceramic and slate is expensive to install but long wearing.

FACING PAGE *For flooring that will deliver lasting good looks, choose quality materials.*

Fine Fabrics

Quality fabrics retain their great looks after lesser materials have given way. Fabric quality is determined by fibre content, weave and pattern. The fabric should also be resistant to fading, shrinking and use.

The fibre content of fabric can be natural, such as silk, cotton, wool, linen or leather; synthetic, such as rayon or polyester; or it can be a blend. Natural fibres tend to have the most luxurious look and feel.

The weave of the fibre adds to both the appearance and durability of the fabric. Plain weave, used for cotton prints, offers the least resistance to daily wear and tear. Twill weave, such as denim, is stronger, more durable and more pliable than plain weave. Satin weave, used in satin and cotton sateen, is heavier still. It drapes well and has the most body.

Fabric patterns can be woven into a fabric or printed on top. A jacquard is a type of woven pattern known for both its beauty and durability. Typical applications include upholstery fabrics, damask linens and brocade. Printed fabrics include calicos, chintz and toile. Even at the high end, printed fabrics will not have the durability of jacquards. You can recognize a jacquard from a print by looking at the "wrong" side of the fabric: jacquards look almost the same on either side, but prints show a pale version of the printed design.

FACING PAGE *Quality fabrics have durability that will ensure years of use and enjoyment.*

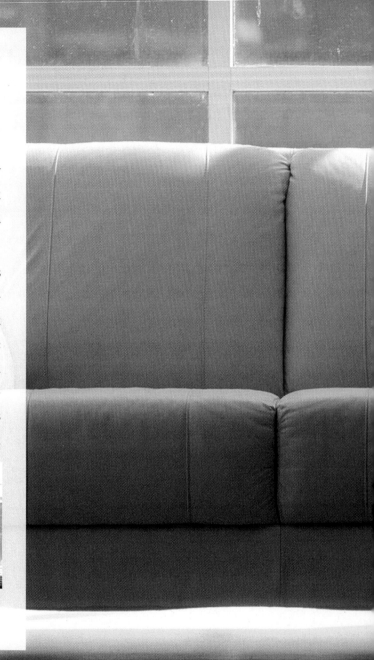

The Luxury of Leather

Literally a second skin, leather is a luxury choice for furnishings that just happens to get better as it ages. Natural hide has a smell, a touch and a look like no other fabric.

Leather is available in a range of grades and finishes for different needs. High protection leather is treated in processing to make it resistant to spills and stains. It's a good choice for heavy-duty family use. Leather covered with a protective finish after tanning safeguards the surface without altering the fabric's natural features. The ultimate is tanned but untreated leather. This natural leather is soft and velvety, and retains natural markings. It ages gracefully, getting softer over the years.

THESE PAGES *A leather couch adds a touch of luxe to this minimal loft space.*

Good Nights

The contents of the linen cupboard were once considered so precious that they were kept under lock and key. What distinguishes fine cloth from the everyday is the type of fibre and the thread count.

The most luxurious bed linens and towels are 100 percent Pima or Egyptian cotton with a high thread count. These cottons have a strength and lustre that makes them look and feel great and last. Pure cotton is also a good choice because of its ability to breathe. With bedding, a thread count of 200-plus usually indicates a fine cotton with a soft hand, or feel. Thread counts in excess of 300 will especially stand up to the rigours of everyday use and laundering.

On beds, the best comforters, blankets and duvets are warm and long-lasting. Comforters should specify bonded fill that will not lump or shift. Wool blankets are a traditional comfort, but many man-made fibres provide warmth while easing the problems with allergies or cleaning that wool can create. For cold nights, duvets are supreme. Down-filled duvets are preferable to feather fills. Canadian goose down is a quality choice. For the crowning touch, a down pillow makes dreams sweet!

THESE PAGES *Beautiful linens deserve to be displayed in a glass-fronted armoire.*

Lasting Quality

Some furnishings capture our imagination. Grandfather clocks, curio cabinets and fine dining room furniture have a timeless quality in every home. They are pieces with history and individuality that will last a lifetime.

Good design and quality craftsmanship are the hallmarks of fine pieces. Period styles such as Chippendale, Sheraton and Empire are still popular for their classic, graceful lines. More recently, the simplicity of Shaker-style, Dutch Colonial and early Canadian furniture has made them sought after both as originals and in reproduction. Each of these classic designs has stood the test of time.

Classic cabinetry is handcrafted of solid wood and hand-rubbed to a fine finish. The wood used in making period-style tables, chairs and bedroom suites is commonly kiln-dried hardwood such as mahogany, walnut, maple, cherry and oak. These particular woods are strong, durable, finish well and take a high polish. Oak is typical of Shaker-style, teak of Dutch Colonial and soft pine of Early Canadian furniture. Teak and pine take on a warm patina and look better as they age.

Quality pieces may be a big investment when first purchased, but their ability to withstand the test of time makes the money well spent.

FACING PAGE *A magnificent four-poster bed is a worthy investment that will be appreciated for years.*

Quality Through and Through

Quality is a choice that can pay for itself many times over. Not only will the furniture last longer, but it will be more comfortable, sturdy and attractive.

Basic to all good furniture is a substantial frame. Quality frames are made from kiln-dried hardwoods. Woods must be free from warping, splitting and swelling and be strong enough to withstand heavy use. The most popular choices are elm, poplar, birch, ash and oak.

Upholstered furniture needs to be well built, inside to out. A good way to test for construction is to sit on the piece. With better furniture, you won't feel the springs or hard edges that can cut into the backs of legs. The cushions should fit together snugly and, if they are reversible, they'll last longer. Unless you have a penchant for fluffing and plumping, opt for comfortable, yet firm, cushions that will better retain their shape. The fabric pattern should be well matched and should run continuously along the side and seat of the piece as well as from top to bottom.

FACING PAGE *Details count when shopping for furnishings.*
TOP LEFT *Look for well padded upholstered arms—the more padding, the better.*
TOP RIGHT *A touch of wood inlay distinguishes fine craftsmanship.*
BOTTOM RIGHT *Upholstery patterns should run continuously from the back to the seat.*
BOTTOM LEFT *Dovetail joints in drawers make for strength.*

Quality Woods

Mahogany is often called the aristocrat of cabinet woods. It is strong, tough and has a lovely finish. Walnut, another sophisticated choice, is sought for its durability and resistance to warping.

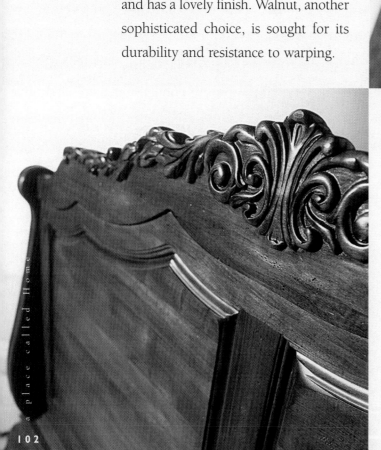

Oak accounts for a large proportion of all wood used in furniture making. It is moderately heavy, hard and strong—characteristics that give it high marks for wear.

Pine is a soft wood with a mellow finish. It marks easily—though the marking adds to its appearance—dries easily and doesn't shrink or swell with changes in humidity.

The merits of solid wood versus veneer (a fine surface layer laminated to particleboard) are often debated. They can be equally beautiful. In fact, it can be difficult to tell from outward appearance which one has been used. In either case, fine craftsmanship will produce a piece that will look good for years.

THESE PAGES

Avoid going against the grain. Choose woods you feel at home with, whether it is a casual wood chair or the finesse of a polished dining table.

Setting the Table

The table is central to your home and should be dressed for the part. What makes for a fine table? For some, it may be a highly formal setting, with fine china, sterling and white linens. For others, a more casual table suits best. For most, it is a combination of both: best quality for special occasions and casual dinnerware for everyday get-togethers.

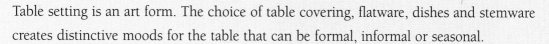

Table setting is an art form. The choice of table covering, flatware, dishes and stemware creates distinctive moods for the table that can be formal, informal or seasonal.

Table coverings establish the degree of formality. Tablecloths are usually more formal, while placemats are used for a less formal setting. Starched white linen, colourful tablecloths and patterned placemats provide a wealth of choice in texture, finish, colour and design.

Your choice of dishes, too, creates a tone. Choose flatware and glasses to accent the dishes. A successful look brings all these elements together so they complement each other and the food being served.

FACING PAGE *This tablecloth and cloth napkins are the starting point for dressing up the table for a casual brunch. The pottery dishes suit the glassware and coloured linens for a relaxed get-together.*

Cook's Desire

Both the materials and the construction of a piece of cookware contribute to its quality.

Stainless steel is highly durable, does not interact with food and will not corrode. Its quality is determined by the ratio of chromium/nickel content. Chromium is a constant factor of 18. The higher the nickel content, the greater the quality.

Stainless steel pots are constructed as single-ply, two-ply and tri-ply. The latter two are excellent conductors of heat and are best used at lower temperatures.

Think about buying for the long term when you purchase kitchenwares. If you choose pots, pans or small appliances that are well made, it's going to make cooking and cleaning up easier and faster. Price is a really good indicator of quality; you'll pretty soon distinguish better made pieces by their solid weight, construction and beautiful finishes.

The best indicators of quality in small appliances are hard surfaces that resist marring; solid, heavy bases that prevent tipovers; multiple-use options and a good warranty that backs strong motors and working parts.

FACING PAGE TOP *Well made saucepans are an excellent long-term kitchen investment.* **BOTTOM** *Stainless steel cookware is highly durable and the choice of many good cooks.* **THIS PAGE TOP** *This chrome-and-glass blender is a classic design made modern again.* **BOTTOM** *Extra-wide slots give this toaster great functionality.*

Table Tops

Tablecloths or placemats are the canvas on which a table is set. Cloths and napkins can range from plain-weave cotton to fine jacquards.

Tablecloths, the more formal option, should fit the table with a generous overhang. Placemats are generally more appropriate for less formal dining. Cork-based mats protect the table and are crisp and sophisticated. For a softer setting, jacquard or quilted-cotton mats fit the bill.

Napkins look best when their texture or design coordinates with the table covering. Napkin rings can add grace to a formal setting or playfulness to a casual setting.

The quality of glassware is determined by its clarity, strength and resiliency. Crystal is actually just a term to describe colourless glass; lead crystal has lead oxide added to the basic crystal mixture. Lead crystal, in itself, is not an indicator of quality because some of the best crystal in the world does not contain lead oxide.

Fine glassware lends elegance to any setting. Use different glasses for different drinks—wines and water—to add variety to the table.

FACING PAGE TOP *Fine tablecloths and napkins add elegance to dining.*
BOTTOM *Bright cotton placemats and napkins make for a cheerful casual table.*
THIS PAGE TOP *Bring out your best: crystal is glassware of the finest quality.*
BOTTOM *Stemmed casual glassware adds a touch of elegence to the everyday table.*

Dish It Up

Bone china, fine china and porcelain are *la crème de la crème* in dishes. Bone china is thin and light. It contains a minimum of 25 percent animal bone ash to give it its characteristic translucency and chalk-white colour. Fine china and porcelain have similar properties in translucency but are off-white or ivory in base colour.

Pottery-based dishes are heavier and more opaque than china. Stoneware, made from light-coloured clay fired at high temperatures, is chip-resistant and ovenproof. A salt glaze gives it a glossy look and granular texture. Earthenware is made from a mix of clay bodies and is glazed in a wide variety of colours. Ironstone is earthenware of good quality.

Hand-painted dishes create one-of-a-kind settings that add charm to the table. Best quality dishes are imprinted with the town or village of origin.

AT RIGHT *Picking dishes is a highly personal exercise. Choose a colour, material and style that suites your lifestyle, complements food and won't become tiresome. Place settings no longer have to be all the same: patterns can be cleverly coordinated for impact.*

A Polished Look

There are three classes of flatware: stainless, silver plate and sterling silver.

Stainless steel flatware with an alloy ratio of 18/8—indicating high nickel content—will keep its colour and lustre.

It has superior resistance to corrosion. Finest quality stainless is a good alternative to silver for formal dining. It is easier to clean and lower maintenance.

Highest quality silver plate has a brass core for superior adhesion. Silver is applied as a veneer over this base. Sterling silver is solid silver, designated by hallmarking on the handles. It has an unmistakable patina that grows more beautiful with age.

Stainless steel kitchen gadgets won't rust and provide great service. It's really worthwhile to spend a bit extra, to get so much more.

Good knives are especially important. They'll save time in the preparation of food, stay sharp longer and be easier to use. Whether you're setting up your first kitchen or you've been cooking for years, an excellent knife is essential.

FACING PAGE *Three classes of flatware are stainless steel, silverplated, and sterling silver.*
THIS PAGE *Stainless steel is a dependable choice for kitchen tools.*

Àu revoir

All merchandise pictured in this book with the exception of vintage items and personal props is available from Sears Canada Inc. Visit one of our stores for more inspiring and affordable ideas for the place you call home.

Special thanks

We'd like to especially thank the management and staff of the following for their help and support in providing merchandise featured in *A Place Called Home*:

Sears Department Stores

Yorkdale Shopping Centre
Dufferin Street
Toronto, ON
416-789-1105

Sherway Gardens
The West Mall
Etobicoke, ON
416-620-6011

Sears Furniture and Appliances Stores

Vega Boulevard
Mississauga, ON
905-820-6801

Sheppard Ave West
North York, ON
416-398-9947

Sears Fall and Winter 2000 General Catalogue

For further product enquiries, please write to:

Sears Whole Home Fashion Office
222 Jarvis Street
7th Floor, D/702M
Toronto, ON
M5B 2B8